Grit

HBR Emotional Intelligence Series

How to be human at work

The HBR Emotional Intelligence Series features smart, essential reading on the human side of professional life from the pages of *Harvard Business Review*.

Authentic Leadership	*Influence and Persuasion*
Confidence	*Leadership Presence*
Dealing with Difficult People	*Mindful Listening*
Empathy	*Mindfulness*
Energy and Motivation	*Power and Impact*
Focus	*Purpose, Meaning, and Passion*
Good Habits	*Resilience*
Grit	*Self-Awareness*
Happiness	*Virtual EI*
Inclusion	

Other books on emotional intelligence from *Harvard Business Review*:

HBR Everyday Emotional Intelligence

HBR Guide to Emotional Intelligence

HBR's 10 Must Reads on Emotional Intelligence

Grit

HBR EMOTIONAL INTELLIGENCE SERIES

Harvard Business Review Press

Boston, Massachusetts

Copyright 2023 Harvard Business School Publishing Corporation

Printed in the UK by TJ Books Limited, Padstow

10 9 8 7 6 5 4 3 2

The web addresses referenced in this book were live and correct at the time of the book's publication but may be subject to change.

Library of Congress Cataloging-in-Publication Data

Names: Harvard Business Review Press, issuing body.
Title: Grit.
Other titles: Grit (Harvard Business Review Press) | HBR emotional
    intelligence series.
Description: Boston, Massachusetts : Harvard Business Review Press,
    [2023] Series: HBR emotional intelligence series | Includes index.
Identifiers: LCCN 2023008728 (print) | LCCN 2023008729 (ebook) | ISBN
    9781647825614 (paperback) | ISBN 9781647825621 (epub)
Subjects: LCSH: Determination (Personality trait) | Employee motivation. |
    Job stress. | Perseverance (Ethics) | Success in business.
Classification: LCC BF698.35.D48 G758 2023 (print) | LCC BF698.35.D48
    (ebook) | DDC 155.2/32--dc23/eng/20230501
LC record available at https://lccn.loc.gov/2023008728
LC ebook record available at https://lccn.loc.gov/2023008729
ISBN: 978-1-64782-561-4
eISBN: 978-1-64782-562-1

The paper used in this publication meets the requirements of the American National Standard for Permanence of Paper for Publications and Documents in Libraries and Archives Z39.48-1992.

Contents

Contents

Contents

Grit

HBR EMOTIONAL INTELLIGENCE SERIES

1

To Build Grit, Go Back to Basics

An interview with Shannon Huffman Polson
by Curt Nickisch

The concept of grit has been growing in popularity in recent years. It's an essential quality for facing stress, pushing through difficulties, and overcoming obstacles both at work and in life. But not everyone has grit, nor do they understand how to build it.

Shannon Huffman Polson knows all about the kind of mental and emotional fortitude that so many experts say people need. She was one of the first women to pilot the Apache attack helicopter in the U.S. Army, has launched a successful corporate and consulting career, and is the author of *The Grit Factor: Courage, Resilience, and Leadership in the Most Male-Dominated Organization in the World.*

In this interview, she discusses how to build grit like a muscle—by recognizing your story, understanding your core purpose, and forcing yourself to do hard things.

Curt Nickisch: *First and foremost, what does* grit *mean to you?*

Shannon Huffman Polson: The way that I have defined it over the years is "a dogged determination in the face of difficult circumstances." Angela Duckworth of the University of Pennsylvania has defined grit as "passion and perseverance toward long-term goals," which I also love. I will say that in today's context—where the future is very uncertain, where the horizon is especially unclear, and where we're all working in these environments that are much more ambiguous—I have a slight preference for my own definition.

Let's talk about your personal experience and understanding of grit. Where did it come from?

It's something that I grew up talking about with my dad especially. It's the term that we would use for pushing through and doing hard things. That has become an important part of who I am and how I've approached life and challenges. As I got older, I also understood that it's something that not everybody had the exposure to and that many, many people were looking for.

How did your father instill this in you?

A lot of the ways that we're able to relay a message or a concept, both as parents and managers, is through stories and through questions.

There's a story that I tell: I was on the soccer field, and my parents were there cheering. This was not the kind of hypercompetitive soccer that people play now. It was Girls' Club soccer. We were all about nine or 10 years old. There was a young woman playing offense on the other team who would just crush the field. We would always part like the Red Sea as she came charging at us, and she would score every single time.

I remember after one game, my dad asked me, "Why don't you just run back at her?" That was a mind-boggling concept. But the next time we played against that team, she came charging down my side of the field, and I went charging back at her. We collided at full speed. She never charged my side of the field again.

There is a combination of things there, but part of it was the willingness to go into something that I was afraid of, that I knew was going to be difficult, that I knew was—in that case—going to hurt. And being willing to do it anyway.

GRIT VERSUS RESILIENCE: WHAT'S THE DIFFERENCE?

By Courtney Cashman

Grit and resilience are often used interchangeably, but are they the same thing? Not really.

Angela Duckworth, author of the bestselling book *Grit*, famously defines *grit* as "passion and perseverance toward long-term goals." Psychologist Heidi Grant offers another take, describing grit as "a willingness to commit to long-term goals, and to persist in the face of difficulty."[a] Others have their own definitions. But the consistent theme running through these interpretations is one of hard determination and persistence—pushing through in the face of challenges and hardships.

Resilience is a bit more nuanced. Andrea Ovans, former editor at *Harvard Business Review*, defines resilience as "the ability to recover from setbacks, adapt well to change, and keep going in the face of adversity."[b] In other words, it's not just moving forward but also picking yourself up after you fall.

(Continued)

It's having the fortitude to keep going, while also analyzing what happened and making appropriate changes for the future. Resilience requires the use of a growth mindset—a concept pioneered by psychologist and Stanford professor Carol Dweck—where you view obstacles and setbacks as learning experiences. So where grit helps you work through difficult situations (and even endure the toughest), resilience helps you bounce back and become even stronger than before.

Both grit and resilience are essential traits for success at work. Fortunately, they can also both be learned.

a. Heidi Grant, "Nine Things Successful People Do Differently," hbr.org, February 25, 2011, https://hbr.org/2011/02/nine-things-successful -people.

b. Andrea Ovans, "What Resilience Means, and Why It Matters," hbr.org, January 5, 2015, https://hbr.org/2015/01/what-resilience -means-and-why-it-matters.

Courtney Cashman is a senior editor at *Harvard Business Review*.

You faced some of this in the military as well. Tell me about your experience facing obstacles as an aspiring pilot in the U.S. Army.

I certainly didn't go into it understanding the challenges. I went into the military—and into Army attack aviation specifically—because I wanted to do something hard and exciting. I was 21 years old. I don't know what you know when you're 21, but fortunately not enough to dissuade you from what might lie ahead.

I approached Army attack aviation with enthusiasm for the opportunity and the job. Of course, once I got into that position and saw the challenges I would face, especially as one of the first women in the role, it was a very different scenario than any that I had ever found myself in. It offered a lot less support and assurance than I had grown up with, for sure.

What did you encounter along the way?

When I was at Duke University, I was an English major and in the Army ROTC. The assumption was that I would then receive my commission in the National Guard going forward. At the end of my senior year, I drove out to Raleigh, North Carolina, to meet with the state aviation officer and receive my assignment for the years ahead.

I remember reporting to a colonel who was probably in his late thirties. He was behind this immense desk that seemed as wide as the room, with shiny windows going up the back. I stood at attention and saluted and tried not to shake too much. He had me take a seat, and we exchanged a couple of pleasantries in a very formal sort of a way before the exchange that I will never forget: He stopped midsentence, leaned back in his chair, looked down his nose at me, and said, "You realize, cadet, that you will never fly an attack aircraft."

I recognized his comment for what it was meant to be, which was small and mean, because at the time—in 1993—attack aircraft weren't open to women to fly. But I also understood in my extremely nascent military career that there are times when the only thing you can say is, "Yes, sir," so I did. Then I went back to the Duke ROTC detachment and requested a transfer out of the National Guard and into active duty.

Later that spring, Congress lifted the combat exclusion clause for aviation. Suddenly, everything in the inventory was open to women *and* men to fly. And I reported to Fort Rucker later that year.

The moment with the colonel—that was a moment where a lot of people would stop, right? Or accept the powers that be?

A big part of what begins the grit-forming process is deciding that *you* are going to be the person in

11

charge of your own story, not someone else. *You* are going to be the person that decides what your narrative will be. You can't choose the raw material, but you can decide how you're going to use it. Many people don't do that.

How do you take that first step?

It's about focusing on your end goal and what your purpose is. When you're focused on that core purpose—that you are going to succeed, that you are going to contribute in this meaningful way—that allows you to not concentrate on the obstacles as much. It's a choice of where you put your focus.

Why is focusing on your own story so important?

The way we understand information, really, is in the form of a story. Thinking back to make sense of our own stories—to understand the places where we grew, to understand our strengths, to understand where we overcame obstacles—becomes part of how we can approach future challenges or even current ones. It's thinking back and saying, "Hey—look at how I got through this really hard time. I either developed that strength or I realized there was a way around this hurdle." Doing that can help you find ways to negotiate the challenges that you're facing today, and that's critical work.

You aren't just making sense of the raw material that you're given. You're looking at how you turned the raw material of your life into your story. Because you get to choose. You get to say either, "I was a victim of this circumstance" or "I was able to overcome this. I was able to push through."

When you do that work and you decide what that arc of that story of your life is going to be, then you can borrow from the strengths of that. You can understand your values and how to go forward in connection with those values in a way that strengthens you for what you might be facing today or will be facing in the future.

You know your own story very well. How do you help people figure out what their story is, so that they know what to commit to?

There are a number of tactical exercises that I suggest. One of them is to start with what is sometimes called a *journey line*, or a *lifeline*: Look at your major life experiences, really own and understand the raw material of them, and get that down on paper. Then, study what you've written, aiming to understand how that relates to and informs your core values and your core purpose.

Another exercise that I love drills down into your core purpose. This is pretty deep internal work; it's not back-of-the-napkin analysis. It requires time and space for you to think about—and to think about again and again. The exercise was developed by Toyota and is called the "Five Whys." Ask yourself why you're doing something, not one time but five times—a *why* for each answer you come up with. Drill down into that deep, deep *why* that's not specific to the job, that's not specific to the task, but that is truly connected to who you are as an individual. You've got to make that strong connection that is uniquely yours before you can apply it to whatever the task is, whatever the company is, whatever the company's missions and values and goals are.

For me, it's service and serving others. Growing up, we made food for people who didn't have enough. We visited retirement homes. The concept of contribution and giving back became a very big part of who I am. Connecting to that purpose allows me to get through times that are difficult, frustrating, or both.

Was there a time in your military career where you faced obstacles and recalling that core idea of service helped you get through them?

The best example I have for this is maybe one of the least exciting, but also one of the most relatable. When I first was assigned to Fort Bragg, North Carolina, it was my first duty assignment and I was 23 years old.

I was qualified to pilot the Apache helicopter. I was excited. I was ready to fly and to lead. But when I arrived in the 229th Aviation Regiment, there were two battalions. There were 120 male pilots, and I was the only female pilot. I was assigned not to a platoon where I would be flying and using the craft that I had just learned, but as the assistant to the assistant operations officer.

A desk job.

Exactly. And not typing up, for example, operations orders where you're getting into the meat of things, but writing the appendixes to the operations orders.

I was brought up believing that you do the best job you can, so I did the best job I could. I had great feedback, and I went to the captain I was working for and said, "Listen, sir. I'm going to keep doing the best job I can at this work, but I wonder when a platoon might open up." That captain looked at me and said, "Lieutenant, the Army doesn't owe you anything."

I kept on doing my work. And then at some point, we were all brought in on a Saturday to do work together as an operations shop for no apparent reason. The major that we all worked for looked over at me and joked, "Don't worry, Lieutenant, you'll be married by the time you're 25."

I did not say, "Yes, sir," as I had to that colonel back in Raleigh. I went to see the major the next week and said, "Sir, I'm going to keep doing the best job I can at what I've been assigned, but I think that I can do more." He looked kind of surprised. Then he assigned me one additional duty after the other. And finally, I took that first flight platoon.

I think back on those times and about how they apply to the people and companies I have the chance to talk to across the country and around the world. I talk to people all the time who don't know how to push back when somebody says, "The Army doesn't owe you anything," or "You'll be married by the time you're 25." They just think that's where they're stuck.

I strongly believe that there's an opportunity for us to push through those things by owning our story, by drilling down into core purpose, and by learning to have the courage to ask for what you want again and again. Every single opportunity that I had in the military, I had to ask for. I had to earn it first, of course—but then I had to ask for it. And that's an important lesson in that whole process.

How do you become better at grit? When you have setbacks or something gets in your way, how do you develop grit then?

There are three different phases. The *commit* phase is what we've already talked about—owning your own story and drilling down to core purpose.

The second phase is *learn*, and the third, *launch*. In that second phase of learning, a few things are important, and this goes to your question. One of them is developing your team, or drawing your circle, because the people who don't support you should be outside of it. But you need to have a team. None of us do this alone. That is critical when times get tough.

Is that a misunderstanding of grit, that it's an individual quality?

Sometimes. A lot of us have had experiences where if we want to get it done well, we do it ourselves. But both the mentality and the reality of that aren't sustainable. It might be something we can do in the short term, but it's not a sustainable solution for the long run.

When you talk about grit—and this goes back to Angela Duckworth's definition—you're talking about "passion and perseverance toward long-term goals." Or, if it's "dogged determination," there's a sustainability aspect to that which has to come into play. You can't do it yourself. You've got to build that team.

But there are very specific ways that you can build grit and resilience. I borrow a lot from the Army's master resilience training program, which was developed at the University of Pennsylvania as part of their positive psychology program. Decades of research have gone into this, and there are very specific things that you can do.

To put one of them in a nutshell: To get better at doing hard things, you need to do hard things. It sounds almost trite to say, but you take one step. You challenge yourself a little bit more the next time, and the next, and the next. That is truly how you build up a muscle for grit and resilience. And it's absolutely something that is accessible to every single one of us.

SHANNON HUFFMAN POLSON is one of the first women to fly the Apache helicopter in the U.S. Army. In addition to her military service, she earned an MBA at the Tuck School of Business at Dartmouth College and spent five years leading and managing in the corporate sector at Guidant and Microsoft. She is the founder of the Grit Institute, the author of *The Grit Factor: Courage, Resilience, and Leadership in the Most Male-Dominated Organization in the World* and the memoir *North of Hope: A Daughter's Arctic Journey*, and speaks frequently on topics related to leadership, courage, resilience, and grit. CURT NICKISCH is a senior editor at *Harvard Business*

Review, where he makes podcasts and cohosts *HBR IdeaCast*. He earned an MBA from Boston University and previously reported for NPR, *Marketplace*, WBUR, and *Fast Company*. He speaks *ausgezeichnet* German and binges history podcasts. Find him on Twitter @CurtNickisch.

Adapted from "To Build Grit, Go Back to Basics," *HBR IdeaCast* (podcast), September 1, 2020.

2

Gauging Your Grit

By Thomas H. Lee and Angela Duckworth

How much grit do you have?

To see how gritty you are compared with a pool of more than 5,000 American adults, answer the questions on the next page, assigning each a number between 1 and 5, where 1 is "very much like me" and 5 is "not at all like me." Tally your score and divide by 10. Don't overthink your answers or try to guess the "right" answer. The more honestly you respond, the more accurate the results.

On a scale of 1–5:
1 = Very much like me
5= Not at all like me

1. New ideas and projects sometimes distract me from previous ones.

_____

2. Setbacks don't discourage me. I don't give up easily.

_____

3. I often set a goal but later choose to pursue a different one.

_____

4. I am a hard worker.

_____

5. I have difficulty maintaining my focus on projects that take more than a few months to complete.

_____

6. I finish whatever I begin.

_____

7. My interests change from year to year.

_____

8. I am diligent. I never give up.

_____

9. I have been obsessed with a certain idea or project for a short time but later lost interest.

_____

10. I have overcome setbacks to conquer an important challenge.

_____

Compare your results with the percentiles below to find out if you have more or less grit than average. If you scored at least 4.5, for instance, you are grittier than 90% of test takers.

Grit score	2.5	3.0	3.3	3.5	3.8	3.9	4.1	4.3	4.5	4.7	4.9
Percentile	10%	20%	30%	40%	50%	60%	70%	80%	90%	95%	99%

THOMAS H. LEE is the chief medical officer of Press Ganey. He is also a professor of health policy and management at the Harvard T.H. Chan School of Public Health and a senior physician at Brigham and Women's Hospital. ANGELA DUCK-WORTH is the Rosa Lee and Egbert Chang Professor at the University of Pennsylvania and the Wharton School. She is also cofounder, chief scientist, and a board member of Character Lab, a nonprofit whose mission is to advance scientific insights that help children thrive.

Excerpted from "Organizational Grit," in *Harvard Business Review*, September–October 2018 (product #R1805G).

3

How to Deal with High-Pressure Situations at Work

By Tomas Chamorro-Premuzic

M any of the things we're proud to achieve in life are the product not just of our talent and effort but also our ability to handle pressure. From studying for exams, to preparing for job interviews, to giving a big speech or presentation, it's hard to conceive of any career-defining moments that aren't peppered with pressure.

One of the oldest findings in modern psychology is that a moderate amount of pressure can actually boost performance.[1] This is why top athletes will generally perform better in competitions than in training, and why professional musicians will be more motivated if they're in front of an audience than rehearsing at home. In general, the more skilled you are at something, the more you're able to translate external or situational pressure into a performance-enhancing ingredient.

That said, when pressure levels exceed our optimal threshold, they can negatively impact our performance. They do so mostly by hijacking our focus and attention (away from the task and onto our negative emotions), lowering our confidence, and causing stress and anxiety.[2] For example, research found that up to 60% of students experience test anxiety during exams, and a whopping 93% of people feel anxious in job interviews.[3] Then there is the fear of public speaking, which ranks as one of the top phobias in the modern world.[4]

What, then, can you do to improve your ability to deal with pressure, or at least avoid choking under it in critical career moments? Here are four science-based recommendations that can help.

Know your threshold

Humans are a psychologically diverse species. One of the traits that makes each of us unique is our ability to deal with stress. Some call this *emotional intelligence*, others call it *grit* or *resilience*. The most widely used academic term for this trait is *emotional stability*. Leaving labels aside, this trait enhances your ability to cope with pressure, making you more cool-headed and less emotionally reactive.

Regardless of your individual personality, the first step to managing high-pressure situations is understanding your stress-tolerance level. Practical tips for building self-awareness include getting feedback from trusted colleagues and friends, evaluating your performance under different degrees of pressure, paying attention to your emotional reactions in potentially triggering situations, and taking a personality assessment (like the one found in chapter 2).

An easy first step is to pick one or two trusted colleagues and ask:

- Do you think I perform well under pressure?

- Do I look nervous or tense in high-stakes situations?

- Do you see any changes in my behavior when I'm under calm or high-pressure situations?

- Do I generally seem calm and composed to you?

The more people you ask, the better the sense you will get of your reputation for dealing with stress and pressure. Your colleagues may even point out specific situations that elicit your stress response—perhaps ones you never noticed before.

Any feedback that tells you something about you that you (a) didn't know and (b) needed rather than wanted to hear is useful feedback. Fundamentally, knowing your personal pressure triggers will help you avoid them, or practice managing your reactions in those moments.

Identify your pressure triggers—and practice

Once you have a better sense of your personality and how it affects or relates to your propensity to deal with pressure, you should be better able to identify the exact triggers that exceed your default comfort levels. Do you get stressed by a high workload or looming deadlines? Does failing to meet your social or family obligations make you anxious? Are there things about your lifestyle—like an unhealthy diet or conflicts with your romantic partner, work colleagues, or relatives—that weigh on you?

While your overall potential to handle pressure will depend primarily on your personality, regardless of how calm or reactive you are, there will be particular situations that evoke more negative reactions than others, and these are very personal and individual. For instance, you may be someone who is never stressed at work but gets easily annoyed by family, or someone who enjoys working with others but is easily stressed by their boss.

Fortunately, we can all learn to minimize situations that put too much pressure on us by planning, prioritizing, picking our battles, and going outside our comfort zones within reason; that is, without going over the tipping point. As with any skill or ability, practice is key, yet it's generally underrated as a means to mitigate and prevent pressure, including on recruitment tests, job interviews, and presentations. Research shows that practice improves the performance in all these instances, mostly by mitigating anxiety.

For example, if you know that your boss is a source of stress for you, assess how you can change your interactions with them. When communicating with your boss, pick a medium you prefer (in person, email, Slack, Zoom, etc.) and the format of the interaction. Schedule a one-on-one meeting in advance so you can prepare, rehearse, and focus. Establish a few points you want to cover in these moments to get what you need to do your job well (what they expect, what you need to deliver, and how you need to communicate).

You may also want to try engaging with your boss on a more casual social basis, such as grabbing lunch or having a virtual coffee. Get to know each other on an informal basis, break the ice, and establish a healthy rapport.

In general, planning ahead of time and establishing communication norms with the people who stress you out will increase the familiarity and predictability of your interactions and decrease the stress and anxiety you feel around them. This is true even for stressful situations that don't revolve around specific people, like public speaking or job interviews. The more predictable you can make the situation, the less stressed you will feel.

Use these strategies to help you cope in the moment

There will obviously be situations in which pressure is unavoidable and your only option is to just move forward. Research shows that if you turn the following practices into daily or weekly habits, your ability to manage pressure when it comes on quickly will improve: breathing exercises, better sleep quality (particularly the night before a high-pressure event), mindfulness and meditation, physical exercise, and thinking techniques such as cognitive reappraisal, whereby you learn to reinterpret a stressful situation as less stressful.[5]

Because caffeine heightens mental arousal, which can worsen anxiety, avoid having too many coffees or energy drinks before a big event. The pressure you feel at any given moment is caused largely by your own thoughts, ideas, and interpretations of things. This is why two people will experience different levels of pressure in the same situation, and why a fast heartbeat could signal either intense physical activity or anxiety. The difference is not what your body does, but what your mind thinks.

Pressure and stress, just like anger or happiness, are mostly states of mind. When stress shows up unexpectedly despite your other efforts, you can de-emphasize the seriousness of the situation by focusing less on yourself, finding something or someone else to focus on, trying to enjoy certain aspects of the situation, and leveraging effective self-presentation, such as showing humor, honesty, or vulnerability.

If you're nervous during a job interview, for instance, you may be better off admitting it right away than trying to hide it or fake confidence. Saying something like, "I'm really sorry, but my nerves are getting to me right now. Forgive me if I take a few deep breaths to relax," may be a better tactic in gaining sympathy than denial or deception. Once you regain your composure, continue to lean on the tactic of honesty: Speak about your interest in the job, opening up about why you're passionate, rather than worrying about performing or making a good impression. After all, if you really care about the job—which would explain your nerves—then finding an honest way to convey it will be impactful.

Remember: Everybody gets nervous, except for those who are overconfident. The people worth working with will prefer humility over narcissism. Don't force yourself to be someone you're not in any scenario. When your nerves come on suddenly, turn your genuine vulnerability into an honest expression of who you are.

Don't avoid pressure entirely

You will want to keep some level of pressure in your life. It will ensure that you develop strength, grit, and resilience; that your competitive instincts get activated; and that you go outside your comfort zone to achieve bigger things. If you're not experiencing any pressure, then you're probably not aiming high enough.

There are plenty of situations that show how feeling too little pressure can impair your performance: being bored at work, being uninterested in impressing others, or doing something that's so easy you don't even have to focus. It's only by testing your limits that you can learn about your talents, stretch yourself mindfully, and develop your potential.

There is no better feedback than failure, and failing at something difficult and meaningful is the best incentive to bounce back and become a better version of yourself.

In short, pressure is an important part of life, and learning to manage it appropriately will benefit you. Although this is more of an art than a science, you can leverage some of these science-based suggestions to practice more effective ways of managing stress and pressure.

TOMAS CHAMORRO-PREMUZIC is the chief innovation officer at ManpowerGroup, a professor of business psychology at University College London and at Columbia University, cofounder of deepersignals.com, and an associate at Harvard's Entrepreneurial Finance Lab. He is the author of *Why Do So Many Incompetent Men Become Leaders? (and How to Fix It)* (Harvard Business Review Press, 2019), upon which his TEDx talk was based. His latest book is *I, Human: AI, Automation, and the Quest to Reclaim What Makes Us Unique* (Harvard Business Review Press, 2023). Find him at www.drtomas.com and follow him on Twitter @drtcp.

Notes

1. Charlotte Nickerson, "The Yerkes-Dodson Law of Arousal and Performance," *Simply Psychology*, November 15, 2021, https://www.simplypsychology.org/what-is-the-yerkes-dodson-law.html.
2. J. Wang et al., "Self-Consciousness and Trait Anxiety as Predictors of Choking in Sport," *Journal of Science and Medicine in Sport* 7, no. 2 (2004): 174–185; Roy F. Baumeister and Carolin J. Showers, "A Review of Paradoxical Performance Effects: Choking Under Pressure in Sports and Mental Tests," *European Journal of Social Psychology* 16, no. 4 (1986): 361–383.

3. Hilary Phan, "A Student's Perspective on Test Anxiety," UCLA Center for Mental Health in Schools, http://smhp.psych.ucla.edu/pdfdocs/testanx.pdf; Sandeep Babu, "93% of People You Interview for a Job Feel Anxious," Small Business Trends, May 11, 2020, https://smallbiztrends.com/2020/05/job-interview-anxiety-survey.html.
4. Babu, "93% of People You Interview."
5. "Relaxation Techniques: Breath Control Helps Quell Errant Stress Response," Harvard Health Publishing, July 6, 2020, https://www.health.harvard.edu/mind-and-mood/relaxation-techniques-breath-control-helps-quell-errant-stress-response; Philippe R. Goldin and James J. Gross, "Effects of Mindfulness-Based Stress Reduction (MBSR) on Emotion Regulation in Social Anxiety Disorder," *Emotion* 10, no. 1 (2010): 83–91; "Exercise and Stress: Get Moving to Manage Stress," Mayo Clinic, August 3, 2022, https://www.mayoclinic.org/healthy-lifestyle/stress-management/in-depth/exercise-and-stress/art-20044469; Allison S. Troy et al., "Seeing the Silver Lining: Cognitive Reappraisal Ability Moderates the Relationship Between Stress and Depressive Symptoms," *Emotion* 10, no. 6 (2010): 783–795.

Adapted from content posted on Ascend, hbr.org, May 25, 2022.

4

How to Convince Yourself to Do Hard Things

By David Rock

A sk anyone how they're feeling these days and chances are they'll reply with some version of "exhausted." We're tired of operating amid uncertainty. We're tired of balancing home and work. We're tired of too much work and too little time.

When we feel like this, our brains want to save mental energy by directing our focus to the most readily available, recallable information to help us make decisions quickly. We often do this by going with our gut and making our best guess.

This is called the *expediency bias*—rushing to judgment without properly considering all the variables. The brain does this because it's much easier to process existing ideas than new ones, a principle known in psychology as *fluency*. The result is that many of us are naturally inclined to do what simply feels right.

The *hedonic* principle also comes into play: We are wired to move toward things that make us feel good and away from things that make us feel uncomfortable.[1] Our brains tag effort as bad because it's hard work. They default to what feels "normal"—the networks that tell us where and how to travel through our daily existence. Those networks are so deep in our thinking that when we're traveling a new and challenging path—regardless of what that path is— our wheels default back to the worn-in grooves.

And yet, we know that hard actions can have tremendous benefits—ones that may not be visible for some time. Think about starting a new exercise routine. Maybe we have an insight (*If I can run a mile, I'll have more energy to play with my young kids*) that generates an impetus for action. Or maybe a doctor told us that we need to change our lifestyle, or an incentive pops up to spur us on.

But when we go for that initial run, it doesn't feel good. Neither does the next run, or the run after that. Our muscles hurt. The schedule keeps us from the quality time we used to spend catching up with friends. The money we've spent on the new activity causes friction in our household. The negatives compound, continuing to signal all the reasons we should go back to the way it was before—when our muscles didn't hurt, when we grabbed drinks with our friends, when we didn't fight with our partners over spending $100 a month on a gym membership.

So, how do we do hard things when our brains are constantly telling us to avoid effort?

First, tackle them when we're in a good mood. Research has shown that when people are upset, they're less likely to try to do hard things.[2] When they're feeling upbeat, however, they're more likely to take on the hard-but-essential tasks that ultimately make life better. One way we can get ourselves in the right mindset is to do what's called "reappraisal," in which we create a shift in our brain of how we *perceive* a task. Reappraisal can be incredibly effective when we choose one simple, sticky word or phrase that labels where we want to be. For example, literally saying to yourself, "I'm going to feel better once I get this new process down on paper," might be enough to get your brain out of an unproductive loop.

Second, we must give our brains the right amount of autonomy. When we have a choice, our brains often want to default to something easy. But we can mitigate that response by challenging ourselves to be innovative and provide incentives. For example, instead of debating whether to make a healthy choice at lunch, ask yourself: *Do I want this fresh salad that's going to give me energy, or this donut that last time caused me to feel sick afterward and made me sleepy?* Put into a work context: *Do I want to experiment with a new project management tool that might make things easier for my team next week, or do I want to stick with the same spreadsheet that a former employee established, which none of us feel great about anyway?*

Finally, we can accomplish hard things by practicing the habits of a growth mindset and notice when we revert to old ways of thinking and behaving. To challenge patterns or systems that enable or inhibit new habits from taking hold, it's helpful to have the support of others. One way to do that is by sharing stories of trying, in a setting where attempts are prized as much as the results. For example, a team of executives recently tried to block off their mornings from meetings to get their best work done. Some individuals thrived, but others preferred to do their deep thinking in the afternoon. A month after experimenting with the schedule, the team decided it wasn't working well because of conflicting time zones. They opted for a different tactic: making only Monday morning free of meetings. By acknowledging the progress made by trying a new habit, the team was able to continue experimenting instead of just reverting back to old ways.

Doing things that feel uncomfortable and like hard work can seem counterintuitive. But by understanding what's going on in your brain instead of in your gut, you can work toward accomplishing hard things and manage your fears better.

DAVID ROCK is cofounder of the NeuroLeadership Institute and author of *Your Brain at Work*.

Notes

1. Maxime Taquet et al., "Hedonism and the Choice of Everyday Activities," *PNAS* 113, no. 35 (2016): 9769–9773.
2. Taquet, "Hedonism and the Choice of Activities."

Adapted from content posted on hbr.org, December 7, 2021
(product #H06Q8Z).

5

"Mentors Were What Helped Me Survive"

An interview with Misty Copeland by Alison Beard

From her first ballet class, at age 13, Misty Copeland set out to be a professional dancer. As a Black girl entering a discipline dominated by white performers and appreciated mostly by white audiences, she knew the odds were stacked against her. But she pressed on, joining American Ballet Theatre (ABT) and in 2015 becoming its first Black female principal dancer. She has broken ground in roles from Clara to Juliet, published several books, pushed for more diversity in the arts, and is building a charitable foundation.

Alison Beard: *Why did you choose ballet as a career?*

Misty Copeland: I love the sense of structure that it gave me at an early age, which has helped me navigate the twists and turns of my life and career, as a dancer, a writer, an activist, and in my production company. Yes, I love performing, and being onstage, but ballet also made me feel that I was a part of something bigger than myself and gave me an outlet and an escape from the circumstances I grew up in. The discipline, the rigor, the sacrifice— those are beautiful things that children in particular should experience, not necessarily to become professionals but to develop as people. Of course, there are many things about the ballet culture that I think need to be reassessed. But ballet gave me so many tools to be a leader in my community. At the heart of this hundreds-of-years-old art form there's a technique and structure that builds that type of person.

You came from a home that was economically unstable at times. You were also a Black girl trying to break into a very white field. When did you realize that you could overcome those challenges and become a professional ballerina?

Because I started at the age of 13, which is very late, it was immediate. That was the plan. I was given an opportunity by my teacher, Cynthia Bradley, with the intent of training to become a professional. Her attitude was: *You have the potential, and I'm going to invest in you because I think you can make the ballet a career.* So the first week into my first class—on a basketball court at the Boys & Girls Club—I wanted to go on to dance for American Ballet Theatre. That was my goal, and within four years I was in New York performing on the stage at Lincoln Center.

That's a lot of pressure for a 13-year-old, particularly when you're dancing with kids who started at age three. How did you cope?

I never saw it as pressure, I think because I was so naive about the ballet world. My family was, too. We were all new to it. But once I was introduced, I thought, *There's no way I can go on without having this in my life.* I was so immersed in it daily, and I was gaining things that I hadn't had access to before, like stability and a release for things I couldn't communicate. It allowed me to blossom and grow, feeling that I was good at something for the first time. It was fun, never like a daunting task. I think I was 14 the first time I saw ABT perform live in Los Angeles, and it was just, *OK, that's it. That's my future.* I was so in love with it that it became something I felt I had to do.

Your rise was very quick. But there were setbacks: your body changing as a late teen, early injuries. How did you push through?

It was extremely difficult. My path was of course unique, but it's common for young athletes and artists to be called prodigies and then have the realities of how they evolve not match expectations. In the ballet world, we might come into the professional sphere between the ages of 16 and 19, and our bodies are still changing, and we're still learning about who we want to be. So we need a better support structure. Mentors were what helped me survive. There are so many dancers who don't—or can't—make it past that hurdle because they don't have people to guide them. I was very fortunate to have people who wanted to be there for me.

How did you find those mentors?

My first ballet teacher, Cynthia Bradley, and Elizabeth Cantine, the public school teacher who introduced me to Cindy, stayed in my corner. But then, once I moved to New York, I had these amazing Black women who came into my life like angels. That's something innate in Black culture: When so few of us are in certain spaces, and opportunities are limited, you want to be there as a support. Victoria Rowell was one of the first. She was an actress, but before that she was a classical dancer in ABT's junior company. She didn't get the opportunity I did, so she ventured into another art form. But she understood that path as a Black woman and reached out to me: When ABT performed in Los Angeles, she left a note for me on the bulletin board at the stage door. She invited me to her home and spoke to me like a human: "I've been there." That opened the doors for understanding

that there were so many others to connect with—
that even though I was the only Black woman in
ABT for the first decade of my career, I shouldn't
feel alone. After that I met Susan Fales-Hill, an
ABT board director. She wanted to be there to
keep my head in the game in a healthy way. And
I've had so many others follow.

*Still, I imagine it must have been tough to be "the
only" for so long. How did you deal with that—and
the weight of having to serve as a role model?*

Yes, during those 10 years, there were microaggres-
sions—sometimes daily—and many times I almost
quit. One of my saving graces, though, was my
ability to step back and watch and learn, especially
from the Black men who came and went through
ABT. I saw how they responded when they didn't
get opportunities, how they interacted with their
white counterparts, and how their careers went. I

learned how to navigate and bring up issues with the artistic staff and be heard and accepted without being too aggressive, which is the label that's put on us. You don't want to go in there angry or upset, because then you're the "angry Black woman." You don't want to cry, because they'll see you as weak or overly emotional. Still, I was very up-front and clear about what I was going through, and I never hid the fact that these things were connected to my race. As my amazing mentors came into my life, I learned even better ways to have those conversations and push the company to do more. The pressure to represent for others came later, once I had more exposure and was a principal dancer.

What did it take to get to that principal dancer role— essentially, the top of your field?

Patience, consistency, allowing myself to be open and vulnerable enough to continue to learn and grow, and staying strong when obstacles were thrown at me—such as when certain roles that I clearly should have been cast in went to others. It was believing that my path was never a straight line or like anyone else's. I didn't allow myself to get down and think, *Wow, I'm way too old to be promoted at this point. There's no chance.* Instead, it was, *Well, I've done all these other things on my own time line, so I'm just going to keep pushing and work to get to where I want to.* It was also having Alexei Ratmansky come in as the choreographer for ABT, see the potential in me, and give me the lead role in his version of *Firebird*—not just following the guidelines that every company does and thinking, *She doesn't fit the mold.* The audience that came in for that because I was Black and young was different from what the ballet world had ever seen before, and it changed the perspective on what I could do for the company.

What advice do you give to the up-and-coming dancers you mentor now?

I just remind them that it's not about the videos you post or the endorsements you get through social media. It's about the work you're putting in. There's no way to go on stage and be the dancer and the artist you want to be if you're not prepared, focused, and grounded.

MISTY COPELAND is a principal dancer at American Ballet Theatre and the author of *New York Times* bestsellers *The Wind at My Back*, *Life in Motion*, *Ballerina Body*, *Black Ballerinas*, and the children's picture book *Bunheads*, as well as the award-winning children's book *Firebird*. ALISON BEARD is an executive editor at *Harvard Business Review* and previously worked as a reporter and editor at the *Financial Times*. Follow her on Twitter @alisonwbeard.

Excerpted from "Life's Work: An Interview with Misty Copeland," in *Harvard Business Review*, July–August 2022 (product #R2204P).

6

When to Grit—
and When to Quit

By André Spicer

When Vontae Davis walked off the football field at halftime in 2018, the Buffalo Bills were down 28-6 to the Los Angeles Chargers. But instead of regrouping with teammates, the Bills cornerback quit football entirely, right then and there. Later that evening, Davis announced his retirement on social media, saying " . . . today on the field, reality hit me hard and fast: I shouldn't be out there anymore." Many were outraged, including Bills linebacker Lorenzo Alexander: "It's just completely disrespectful to his teammates." But some disagreed, saying Davis was "a goddamn working class hero."[1]

While unorthodox, Davis's abrupt midgame retirement sparked strong emotions for a variety of reasons, including a question many of us ask: *How long should I stick with something?* Fortunately, we don't have to rely on NFL commentators to find answers to this question.

Perseverance has received lots of support in recent years from a variety of schools of research. One is from psychologists studying grit. They have found that the capacity to stick to a task—particularly when faced with difficulties—is a crucial factor in explaining the success of everyone from kids in the national spelling bee to recruits at West Point to Ivy League undergraduates.[2]

Then there's the idea that persevering in the face of adversity can prompt learning and improvements of skills. Carol Dweck's work on growth mindsets has found that those who treat challenges and limitations as an opportunity to develop and learn tend to perform better in the long term. They persist when they face challenges, and the reward is a deeper and wider skill set.

Other research challenges these findings, however. One meta-analysis of studies of over 66,000 people found that there was only a moderate correlation between grit and performance.[3] Another study of over 5,600 students taking scholastic aptitude tests found that there was no link between growth mindsets and test scores.[4] People with a growth mindset were not more likely to improve if they took the test again, nor were they more likely to even try to take it again.

In fact, there's a large body of work showing that perseverance may have a harmful downside. Not giving up can mean that people persist even when they have nothing to gain. In one study, people working on an online platform were given a very boring task.[5] The researchers found those who said they were very persistent continued to do the task despite the fact it was boring and there was little to be gained in terms of monetary reward. So while it might be valuable to persist with worthwhile and rewarding tasks, people who don't quit often continue with worthless tasks that are both uninteresting and unrewarding, ultimately wasting their time and talents.

Remaining fixated on long-cherished goals can also mean people ignore better alternatives. A great example of this are Minor League Baseball players.[6] These players often receive low pay and have little job security, but live in hope of being spotted and making it into the major leagues. Only about 11% of players will make that transition. The other 89% are left languishing for years. If they stopped playing baseball, they would be more likely to find alternative employment that was more secure, paid more, and had a more defined career path. In short, by remaining under the spell of their dream, they are unable to explore other options that might be more lucrative.

Being unwilling to let go can lead to people being perpetually dissatisfied—even when they end up getting what they thought they wanted. This was nicely illustrated in a study of graduating college students searching for a job.[7] The researchers found that students who had a tendency to "maximize" their options and were fixated on achieving the best possible job possible did end up getting 20% more in terms of salary. However, they were generally more dissatisfied with the job they got, and they found the process of getting the job more painful.

An unwillingness to quit can be more than just unrewarding. In some situations, it can become downright dangerous. This happens when people's persistence leads them to continue with, or even double down on, losing courses of action. One study found that people who were particularly gritty were less likely to give up when they were failing.[8] These same people were more likely to be willing to suffer monetary losses just so they could continue doing a task. Another study of would-be inventors found that over half would continue with their invention even after receiving reliable advice that it was fatally flawed, sinking more money into the project in the process.[9] The lesson: People who tend to be tenacious are also those who get trapped into losing courses of action.[10]

Being unable to let go of cherished but unachievable goals can also be bad for your mental and physical health.[11] People who struggle to disengage with impossible goals tend to feel more stress, show more symptoms of depression, be plagued by intrusive thoughts, and find it difficult to sleep. They have higher rates of eczema, headaches, and digestion issues. Being fixated on unachievable goals is also related to high levels of cortisol (which over time is linked with things like weight gain, high blood pressure, negative mood, and sleeping problems) and higher levels of C-reactive protein (which is linked with inflammation in the body).

So when you ask yourself whether to stick with a task or goal or to let it go, weigh the potential to continue learning and developing incrementally against the costs, dangers, and myopia that can come with stubborn perseverance.

ANDRÉ SPICER is a professor of organizational behavior at Cass Business School in London and the author of *Business Bullshit*.

Notes

1. Adam Stites, "Vontae Davis Had a Good Reason for Retiring at Halftime of the Bills Game," SBNation, September 19, 2018, https://www.sbnation.com/2018/9/16/17867470/vontae-davis-bills-retired-quit; Matt Stevens and Jason M. Bailey, "Vontae Davis of Buffalo Bills Retires During an NFL Game," *New York Times*, September 16, 2018, https://www.nytimes.com/2018/09/16/sports/football/vontae-davis-halftime-retirement.html; Ryan Van Bibber, "Vontae Davis Quitting in the Middle of a Game Makes Him a Goddamn Working Class Hero," SBNation, September 17, 2018, https://www.sbnation.com/nfl/2018/9/17/17869260/vontae-davis-retired-quitting-buffalo-bills-middle-of-a-game-working-class-hero.

2. Angela L. Duckworth et al., "Grit: Perseverance and Passion for Long-Term Goals," *Journal of Personality and Social Psychology* 92, no. 6 (2007): 1087–1101.

3. Marcus Credé, Michael C. Tynan, and Peter D. Harms, "Much Ado About Grit: A Meta-analytic Synthesis of the Grit Literature," *Journal of Personality and Social Psychology* 113, no. 3 (2017): 492–511.

4. Štěpán Bahník and Marek A. Vranka, "Growth Mindset Is Not Associated with Scholastic Aptitude in a Large Sample of University Applicants," *Personality and Individual Differences* 117, no. 15 (2017): 139–143.

5. Torleif Halkjelsvik and Jostein Rise, "Persistence Motives in Irrational Decisions to Complete a Boring Task," *Personality and Social Psychology Bulletin* 41, no. 1 (2014): 90–102.

6. Stephen Dubner, "Freakonomics: When It's Good to Quit," *Marketplace* (podcast), June 28, 2011, https://www.marketplace.org/2011/06/28/life/freakonomics-radio/freakonomics-when-its-good-quit/.

7. Sheena S. Iyengar et al., "Doing Better but Feeling Worse: Looking for the 'Best' Job Undermines Satisfaction," *Psychological Science* 17, no. 2 (2006): 143–150.

8. Gale M. Lucas et al., "When the Going Gets Tough: Grit Predicts Costly Perseverance," *Journal of Research in Personality* 59 (2015): 15–22.

9. Thomas B. Astebro, Scott A. Jeffrey, and Gordon K. Adomdza, "Inventor Perseverance After Being Told to Quit: The Role of Cognitive Biases," *Journal of Behavioral Decision Making* 20, no. 3 (2007): 253–272.

10. Larbi Alaoui and Christian Fons-Rosen, "Know When to Fold 'Em: The Flip Side of Grit," Universitat Pomeu Fabra working paper no. 1521, April 2016, https://repositori.upf.edu/bitstream/handle/10230/26833/1521.pdf.

11. Carsten Wrosch, Michael F. Scheier, and Gregory E. Miller, "Goal Adjustment Capacities, Subjective Well-Being, and Physical Health," *Social and Personality Psychology Compass* 7, no. 12 (2013): 847–860.

Adapted from "When to Stick with Something—and When to Quit," on hbr.org, September 28, 2018 (product #H04K7S).

7

Are You Pushing Yourself Too Hard?

By Rebecca Zucker

We all have intense periods at work where multiple deadlines converge, an important deal is closing, or a busy season lasts for a few months. During these times, we may work more intensely or put in longer hours, but we know that the situation is temporary, and we are able to keep work in perspective. Conversely, approximately 10% of Americans are considered workaholics, defined as having a "stable tendency to compulsively and excessively work."[1]

Whether you are in the midst of a temporary work crunch or if working all the time is your version of "normal," there are some key signs that you are pushing yourself too hard.

You aren't taking time off

Consistently putting off vacations (including working over major holidays), regularly working all weekend, or dismissing the idea of an occasional day—or even part of a day—off is a sign that you are burning the candle from both ends. While only 23% of Americans take their full allotted vacation time, studies of elite athletes show that taking rest periods is precisely what helps them to perform at full throttle when needed. And the same is true for the rest of us.[2] While extended vacations are helpful, smaller breaks—such as taking the weekend to recharge, carving out personal time in the evening, or having an occasional day off—can also be an important part of having sufficient downtime to restore your energy and counter the drain of being "always on."

You deprioritize personal relationships

When we focus exclusively on work for extended periods, it often comes at the expense of our personal relationships. During 2018, for instance, 76% of U.S. workers said that workplace stress affected their personal relationships, with workaholics being twice as likely to get divorced.[3]

Not taking time to connect with friends and family can also be detrimental to our health. Research shows that strong social relationships are positively correlated to lifespan and that a lack of social relationships has the same effect as smoking 15 cigarettes a day.[4] If you are not taking time outside of work to connect socially with others and have become increasingly isolated, such that social invitations have dried up because others assume you are not available, chances are you are too focused on work.

You're unable to be fully present outside of work

Another sign you are pushing yourself too hard is that when you *do* leave the office and take time to be with the people you care about, you are not able to mentally turn work off and be present with them. For example, Jeff, a former client of mine who is a senior partner at his law firm, has never gone on vacation without his laptop. In addition, after making a point to spend time on the weekends to connect with his daughter, he confessed to constantly thinking about work and admitted that he couldn't help but compulsively check email on his phone every few minutes.

While it's normal to think about work periodically, it becomes a problem when we're not able to manage our urge to give into work-related distractions, slowly eroding our most important relationships. In his book *Indistractable,* author Nir Eyal points out that these distractions make the people we care about "residual beneficiaries" of our attention, meaning they get what is left over, which is typically not very much.

You're neglecting personal care

This is not the occasional skipping a shower when working from home in your sweatpants. Failing to get sufficient sleep, missing meals or existing on a diet of coffee and energy bars, or abandoning exercise or personal hygiene for extended periods are all indications that you are in an unhealthy behavior pattern. In particular, when we sacrifice sleep for work, we are effectively working against ourselves, as sleep deprivation is shown to impair higher-level cognitive functions including judgment, critical thinking, decision-making, and organization.[5]

Likewise, skipping exercise puts us at a further disadvantage. Exercise has been shown to lower stress, improve mood and energy levels, and enhance cognitive functions such as memory, concentration, learning, mental stamina, and creativity.[6] As a former investment banker who worked 80- to 100-hour weeks during more intense periods, taking breaks to exercise, eat, and even nap in one of the onsite sleeping rooms was critical to maintaining my health, stamina, and productivity.

You see your value as a person completely defined by work

Failure to see a broader perspective, both in terms of how you see your value as a person as well as how you see the importance of work relative to the rest of your life, can be a sign that you are pushing yourself too hard. This myopia is usually driven by deeply held limiting beliefs that create a contracted worldview.

Elisa, the head of engineering at a tech company, pushed herself and her team incredibly hard. Her behavior was driven by a belief that *My value is what I produce*. To broaden her perspective, she asked others she respected about what they valued about her, as well as how they valued themselves. She was able to see not only that people valued her for other things like being a good friend, parent, or thought partner, but also that they defined their own value more broadly than their work.

Sometimes, it takes a big life event—like the birth of a child or the death of a colleague or loved one— to shake someone out of this restricted perspective. Another way to broaden your perspective in the absence of these events is to have interests outside of work, which can be a good reminder that work isn't everything.

While we all need to shift into high gear from time to time, keeping work in perspective with the rest of our lives and taking care of ourselves and our relationships are key to achieving long-term success, both personally and professionally.

REBECCA ZUCKER is an executive coach and a founding partner at Next Step Partners, a leadership development firm. Her clients have included Amazon, Clorox, Morrison Foerster, Norwest Venture Partners, The James Irvine Foundation, and high-growth technology companies like DocuSign and Dropbox. You can follow her on Twitter @rszucker.

Notes

1. Mark D. Griffiths, "Work Addiction and 'Workaholism,'" *Psychology Today*, February 12, 2018, https://www .psychologytoday.com/us/blog/in-excess/201802/work -addiction-and-workaholism; Cecilie Schou Andreassen, "Workaholism: An Overview and Current Status of the Research," *Journal of Behavioral Addictions* 3, no. 1 (2014): 1–11.

2. Julia Horowitz, "Americans Gave Up Half of Their Vacation Days Last Year," CNN Money, May 25, 2017, https://money.cnn.com/2017/05/24/news/vacation-days-unused/index.html; Brad Stulberg and Steve Magness, "How Extended Breaks in Training Help Elite Athletes—and Why You Should Take Them Too," *Sports Illustrated*, June 7, 2017, https://www.si.com/edge/2017/06/07/peak-performance-book-extended-breaks-rest-workouts.

3. "Workplace Stress Continues to Mount," Korn Ferry, n.d., https://www.kornferry.com/insights/this-week-in-leadership/workplace-stress-motivation; "How to Survive a Workaholic Spouse," *Forbes*, December 9, 2008, https://www.forbes.com/2008/12/09/workaholic-marriage-divorce-ent-hr-cx_ml_1209workaholicspouse.html.

4. "5 Benefits of Healthy Relationships," Northwestern Medicine, September 2021, https://www.nm.org/healthbeat/healthy-tips/5-benefits-of-healthy-relationships.

5. Lisa Steakley, "What Are the Consequences of Sleep Deprivation?" *Scope*, July 11, 2013, https://scopeblog.stanford.edu/2013/07/11/what-are-the-consequences-of-sleep-deprivation/.

6. Ron Friedman, "Regular Exercise Is Part of Your Job," hbr.org, October 3, 2014, https://hbr.org/2014/10/regular-exercise-is-part-of-your-job.

Adapted from "Are You Pushing Yourself Too Hard at Work?" on hbr.org, January 3, 2020 (product #H05C9Y).

8

How to Cultivate Gratitude, Compassion, and Pride

By David DeSteno

As a leader, what traits should you cultivate in your employees? Grit—the ability to persevere in the face of challenges? Sure. A willingness to accept some sacrifices and work hard toward a successful future are essential for the members of any team. But I believe there's another component that matters just as much: *grace*. I don't mean the ability to move elegantly or anything religious. Rather, I mean qualities of decency, respect, and generosity, all of which mark a person as someone with whom others want to cooperate.

Consider the results of Google's Project Oxygen, a multiyear research initiative designed to identify the manager qualities that enhanced a team's success.[1] What they found is that, yes, driving a team to be productive and results-oriented mattered, but so did being even-keeled, making time for one-on-one meetings, working with a team in the trenches to solve problems, and taking an interest in employees' social lives. In fact, these "character" qualities outranked sheer drive and technical expertise when it came to predicting success.

This makes sense. Innovation typically requires team effort. Expertise has to be combined to solve problems, necessitating cooperation. And cooperation requires a willingness to share credit and support one another as opposed to always striving to take credit for oneself.

So as a manager, what's the best way to instill grit and grace in your team? My research shows that it's about cultivating three specific emotions: gratitude, compassion, and pride.

These three emotions not only increase patience and perseverance but also build social bonds. For most of human evolutionary history, the ability to succeed rested almost entirely on the ability to form relationships. People needed to be honest, fair, and diligent—qualities that required a willingness to inhibit selfish desires to profit at the expense of others. And it was moral emotions like gratitude, compassion, and authentic pride that motivated these actions. For example, research has shown that when people feel grateful, they're willing to devote more effort to help others, to be loyal even at a cost to themselves, and to split profits equally with partners rather than take more money for themselves.[2] When they feel compassion, they're willing to devote time, effort, and money to aid others.[3] And when they feel proud—an authentic pride based on their abilities as opposed to a hubristic one—they'll work harder to help colleagues solve problems.[4] And all of these behaviors draw others to us. People who express gratitude, compassion, and pride are viewed positively by those around them.[5]

These emotions also build grit. They increase the value people place on future goals relative to present ones, and thereby pave the way to perseverance. Work from my lab, for example, shows that people induced to feel grateful show double the patience when it comes to financial rewards.[6] They're twice as willing to forgo an immediate smaller profit so that they can invest it for a longer-term gain. In a similar vein, people made to feel pride or compassion are willing to persevere more than 30% longer on challenging tasks compared to those feeling other positive emotions, such as happiness, precisely because pride and compassion induce them to place greater value on future rewards.[7]

Unlike using willpower to keep your nose to the grindstone, using these emotions also helps solve an increasingly common problem of professional life:

loneliness. Today, loneliness has become an epidemic in the United States, with 53% of American workers regularly reporting feeling isolated in their public lives—an immense problem, given the toll loneliness takes on both physical and mental health.[8] Regularly feeling gratitude, compassion, and pride—because these emotions automatically make people behave in more communal and supportive ways—builds social connections. For example, people assigned to engage in simple interventions to feel and express gratitude show enhanced feelings of social connection and relationship satisfaction over time.[9]

Because of the connection between these emotions and grit and social connection, managers who cultivate gratitude, compassion, and pride in their team will see increased productivity and well-being of their workers. As one example, Adam Grant and Francesca Gino, professors at the Wharton School and Harvard Business School, respectively, examined perseverance in an environment that is rife with more rejection than almost any other: fundraising.[10] Over a two-week period, they recorded the number of calls fundraisers made to solicit donations for a university. Between the first and second week, however, half of the fundraisers received a visit from the university's director of annual giving, during which she expressed her appreciation for their work. To get a sense of how this expression of gratitude affected the fundraisers, Gino and Grant had them report how valued and appreciated they felt by their superiors.

Whereas the average performance of both groups had been virtually the same during the first week of the study, those who had heard the grateful message upped their fundraising efforts by 50% during the second week. What's particularly interesting here is the way the benefits of gratitude and pride can feed off one another. In another study on fundraisers, Grant and Amy Wrzesniewski of Yale University found that the gratitude managers expressed toward their employees stoked the employees' pride, which in turn bolstered their efforts.[11]

Compassion, too, builds dedication. Surveying over 200 people working in different units within a large long-term care facility, professors Sigal Barsade and Mandy O'Neil found that those who worked in units characterized by higher feelings of social attachment, trust, acceptance, and support—a composite that could easily be called empathy and compassion—showed not only superior performance and engagement but also increased work satisfaction, less exhaustion, and lower absenteeism.[12]

Gratitude, compassion, and pride make us more willing to cooperate with and invest in others. But because they accomplish this feat by increasing the value the mind places on future gains, they also nudge us to invest in our own futures. In so doing, they make both teams, and the individuals who comprise them, more successful and resilient.

DAVID DESTENO is a professor of psychology at Northeastern University and the author of *Emotional Success: The Power of Gratitude, Compassion, and Pride.*

Notes

1. David A. Garvin, "How Google Sold Its Engineers on Management," *Harvard Business Review*, December 2013, https://hbr.org/2013/12/how-google-sold-its-engineers -on-management.
2. Monica Y. Bartlett and David DeSteno, "Gratitude and Prosocial Behavior," *Psychological Science* 17, no. 4 (2006): 319–325; Monica Y. Bartlett et al., "Gratitude: Prompting Behaviours That Build Relationships," *Cognition and Emotion* 26, no. 1 (2010): 2–13; David DeSteno et al., "Gratitude as Moral Sentiment: Emotion-Guided Cooperation in Economic Exchange," *Emotion* 10, no. 2 (2010): 289–293.
3. David DeSteno, "Compassion and Altruism: How Our Minds Determine Who Is Worthy of Help," *Current Opinion in Behavioral Sciences* 3 (2015): 80–83.
4. David DeSteno, "The Connection Between Pride and Persistence," hbr.org, August 22, 2016, https://hbr.org/2016/ 08/the-connection-between-pride-and-persistence.
5. Sara B. Algoe, Jonathan Haidt, and Shelly L. Gable, "Beyond Reciprocity: Gratitude and Relationships in Everyday Life," *Emotion* 8, no. 3 (2008): 425–429; Susan Sprecher and Pamela C. Regan, "Liking Some Things (in

Some People) More Than Others: Partner Preferences in Romantic Relationships and Friendships," *Journal of Social and Personal Relationships* 19, no. 4 (2016): 463–481; Lisa A. Williams and David DeSteno, "Pride: Adaptive Social Emotion or Seventh Sin?" *Psychological Science* 20, no. 3 (2009): 284–288.

6. David DeSteno et al., "Gratitude: A Tool for Reducing Economic Impatience," *Psychological Science* 25, no. 6 (2014): 1262–1267.

7. Lisa A. Williams and David DeSteno, "Pride and Perseverance: The Motivational Role of Pride," *Journal of Personality and Social Psychology* 94, no. 6 (2008): 1007–1017; Juliana G. Breines and Serena Chen, "Self-Compassion Increases Self-Improvement Motivation," *Personality and Social Psychology Bulletin* 38, no. 9 (2012): 1133–1143.

8. Vivek Murthy, "Work and the Loneliness Epidemic," hbr .org, September 26, 2017, https://hbr.org/2017/09/work -and-the-loneliness-epidemic; Felice J. Freyer, "'Loneliness Kills': Former Surgeon General Sounds Alarm on Emotional Well-Being," *Boston Globe*, January 16, 2018, https://www.bostonglobe.com/metro/2018/01/16/former -surgeon-general-sounds-alarm-hidden-toll-loneliness/ GweBtw1woQyll1Tl8CYpVL/story.html.

9. Robert A. Emmons and Michael E. McCullough, "Counting Blessings Versus Burdens: An Experimental Investigation of Gratitude and Subjective Well-Being in Daily Life," *Journal of Personality and Social Psychology* 84, no. 2 (2003): 377–389; Sara B. Algoe, Barbara L. Fredrickson,

and Shelly L. Gable, "The Social Functions of the Emotion of Gratitude via Expression," *Emotion* 13, no. 4 (2013): 605–609.

10. "The Big Benefits of a Little Thanks," *HBR IdeaCast* (podcast), episode 380, November 27, 2013, https://hbr.org/podcast/2013/11/the-big-benefits-of-a-little-t.

11. Adam M. Grant and Amy Wrzesniewski, "I Won't Let You Down . . . or Will I? Core Self-Evaluations, Other-Orientation, Anticipated Guilt and Gratitude, and Job Performance," *Journal of Applied Psychology* 95, no. 1 (2010): 108–121.

12. Sigal Barsade and Olivia A. O'Neill, "Employees Who Feel Love Perform Better," hbr.org, January 13, 2014, https://hbr.org/2014/01/employees-who-feel-love-perform-better.

Adapted from "How to Cultivate Gratitude, Compassion, and Pride on Your Team," on hbr.org, February 20, 2018 (product #H046D1).

9

Organizational Grit

By Thomas H. Lee and Angela Duckworth

Ｈigh achievers have extraordinary stamina. Even if they're already at the top of their game, they're always striving to improve. Even if their work requires sacrifice, they remain in love with what they do. Even when easier paths beckon, their commitment is steadfast. We call this remarkable combination of strengths *grit*.

Grit predicts who will accomplish challenging goals. Research done at West Point, for example, shows that it's a better indicator of which cadets will make it through training than achievement test scores and athletic ability. Grit predicts the likelihood of graduating from high school and college and performance in stressful jobs such as sales. Grit also, we believe, propels people to the highest ranks of leadership in many demanding fields.

In health care, patients have long depended on the grit of individual doctors and nurses. But in modern medicine, providing superior care has become so complex that no lone practitioner, no matter how driven, can do it all. Today great care requires great collaboration—gritty teams of clinicians who all relentlessly push for improvement. Yet it takes more than that: Health care institutions must exhibit grit across the entire provider system.

In this article, drawing on Tom's decades of experience as a clinician and health care leader and Angela's foundational studies on grit, we've integrated psychological research at the individual level with contemporary perspectives on organizational and health care cultures. As we'll show, in the new model of grit in health care—exemplified by leading institutions like Mayo Clinic and Cleveland Clinic—passion for patient well-being and perseverance in the pursuit of that goal become social norms at the individual, team, and institutional levels. Health care, because it attracts so many elite performers and is so dependent on teamwork, is an exceptionally good place to find examples of organizational grit. But the principles outlined here can be applied in other business sectors as well.

Developing individuals

For leaders, building a gritty culture begins with selecting and developing gritty individuals. What should organizations look for? The two critical components of grit are passion and perseverance. Passion comes from intrinsic interest in your craft and from a sense of purpose—the conviction that your work is meaningful and helps others. Perseverance takes the form of resilience in the face of adversity as well as unwavering devotion to continuous improvement.

The kind of single-minded determination that characterizes the grittiest individuals requires a clearly aligned hierarchy of goals. Consider what such a hierarchy might look like for a cardiologist, as shown in figure 1: At the bottom would be specific tasks on her short-term to-do list, such as meetings to review cases. These low-level goals are a means to an end, helping the cardiologist accomplish midlevel goals, such as coordinating patients' care with other specialists and team members. At the top would be a goal that is abstract, broad, and important—such as increasing patients' quality and length of life. This overarching goal gives meaning and direction to everything a gritty individual does. Less gritty people, in contrast, have less coherent goal hierarchies—and often, numerous conflicts among goals at every level.

It's important to note that assembling a group of gritty people does not necessarily create a gritty organization. It could instead yield a disorganized crowd of driven individuals, each pursuing a separate

FIGURE 1

A cardiologist's goal hierarchy

In this simplified illustration, immediate, concrete goals sit at the bottom. These support broader goals at the next level, which in turn support an overarching primary goal that provides meaning and direction.

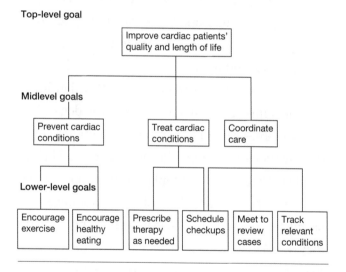

Top-level goal

Improve cardiac patients' quality and length of life

Midlevel goals

Prevent cardiac conditions

Treat cardiac conditions

Coordinate care

Lower-level goals

Encourage exercise

Encourage healthy eating

Prescribe therapy as needed

Schedule checkups

Meet to review cases

Track relevant conditions

passion. If everyone's goals aren't aligned, a culture won't be gritty. And, as we'll discuss in more detail later, it takes effort to achieve that alignment.

Take Mayo Clinic. It is unambivalently committed to a top-level goal of putting patients' needs above all else. It lays out that goal in its mission statement and diligently reinforces it when recruiting. Mayo observes outside job candidates for two to three days as they practice and teach, evaluating not just their skills but also their values—specifically, whether they have a patient-centric mission. Once hired, new doctors undergo a three-year evaluation period. Only after they've demonstrated the needed talent, grit, and goal alignment are they considered for permanent appointment.

How can you hire for grit? Questionnaires are useful for research and self-reflection, but because they're easy to game, we don't recommend using them as hiring tools. Instead, we recommend carefully reviewing an applicant's track record. In particular, look for multiyear commitments and objective evidence of advancement and achievement, as opposed to frequent lateral moves, such as shifts from one specialty to another. When checking references, listen for evidence that candidates have bounced back from failure in the past, demonstrated flexibility in dealing with unexpected obstacles, and sustained a habit of continuous self-improvement. Most of all, look for signs that people are driven by a purpose bigger than themselves, one that resonates with the mission of your organization.

Mayo, like many gritty organizations, develops most of its own talent. More than half the physicians hired at its main campus in Rochester, Minnesota, for example, come from its medical school or training programs. One leader there told us those programs are seen as "an eight-year job interview." When expanding to other regions, both Mayo and Cleveland Clinic prefer to transfer physicians trained within their systems rather than hire local doctors who may not fit their culture.

Creating the right environment can help organizations develop employees with grit. (The idea of cultivating passion and perseverance in adults may seem naive, but abundant research shows that character continues to evolve over a lifetime.) The optimal environment will be both demanding and supportive. People will be asked to meet high expectations, which will be clearly defined and feasible though challenging. But they'll also be offered the psychological safety and trust, plus tangible resources, that they need to take risks, make mistakes, and keep learning and growing.

At Cleveland Clinic, physicians are on one-year contracts, which are renewed—or not—on the basis of their annual professional reviews (APRs). These include a formal discussion of career goals. Before an APR, each of the clinic's 3,600 physicians completes an online assessment, reflects on their progress over the past year, and proposes new objectives for the year ahead. At the meetings, physicians and their supervisors agree on specific goals, such as improving communication skills or learning new techniques. The clinic then offers relevant courses or training along with the financial support and "protected time" the physicians might need to complete it. Improvement is encouraged not by performance bonuses but by giving people detailed feedback about how they're doing on a host of metrics, including efficiency at specific procedures and patient experience. The underlying assumption is that clinicians want to improve and that the organization, and their supervisors in particular, fully backs their efforts to reach targets that may take a year or more to reach.

Building teams

Gritty teams collectively have the same traits that gritty individuals do: a desire to work hard, learn, and improve; resilience in the face of setbacks; and a strong sense of priorities and purpose.

In health care, teams are often defined by the population they serve (say, patients with breast cancer) or the site where they work (the coronary care unit). Gritty team members may have their own professional goal hierarchies, but each will embrace the team's high-level goal—typically, a team-specific objective, such as "improve our breast cancer patients' outcomes," that in turn supports the organization's overarching goal.

Many people in health care associate commitment to a team with the loss of autonomy—a negative—but gritty people view it as an opportunity to provide better care for their patients. They see the whole as greater than the sum of its parts, recognizing that they can achieve more as a team than as individuals.

In business, teams are increasingly dispersed and virtual, but the grittiest health care teams we've seen emphasize face-to-face interaction. Members meet frequently to review cases, set targets for improvement, and track progress. In many instances the entire team discusses each new patient. These meetings reinforce the sense of shared purpose and commitment and help members get to know one another and build trust—another characteristic of effective teams.

That's an insight that many health care leaders have come to by studying the description of the legendary six-month Navy SEAL training in *Team of Teams*, by General Stanley McChrystal. As he notes, the training's purpose is "not to produce super-soldiers. It is to build superteams." He writes, "Few tasks are tackled alone . . . The formation of SEAL teams is less about preparing people to follow precise orders than it is about developing trust and the ability to adapt within a small group." Such a culture allows teams to perform at consistently high levels, even in the face of unpredictable challenges.

Commitment to a shared purpose, a focus on constant improvement, and mutual trust are all hallmarks of integrated practice units (IPUs)—the gold standard in team health care. These multidisciplinary units provide the full cycle of care for a group of patients, usually those with the same condition or closely related conditions. Because IPUs focus on well-defined segments of patients with similar needs, meaningful data can be collected on their costs and outcomes. That means that the value a unit creates can be measured, optimized, and rewarded. In other words, IPUs can gather the feedback they need to keep getting better.

UCLA's kidney transplant IPU is a prime example. Two years after the 1984 passage of the National Organ Transplant Act, which required organ transplant programs to collect and report data on outcomes such as one-year success rates, Kaiser Permanente approached UCLA about contracting for kidney transplantation. This dominant HMO would increase its referrals to UCLA if UCLA would accept a fixed price for the entire episode of care (a "bundled payment"). After taking the deal, UCLA had an imperative to deliver great outcomes (or risk public humiliation and loss of referrals) and be efficient (or risk losing money under the bundled payment contract).

The team has grown to be one of the largest in the country, and its success rates (risk-adjusted patient and graft survival) have been significantly higher than national benchmarks almost every year. With medical advances and public reporting, kidney transplantation success rates have improved across the country—but UCLA has stayed at the front of the pack.

Gritty organizations

If gritty individuals and teams are to thrive, organizations need to develop cultures that make them, in turn, macrocosms of their best teams and people.

So organizations benefit from making their goal hierarchies explicit. If an organization declares that it has multiple missions, and can't prioritize them, it will have difficulty making good strategic choices.

Another danger is promoting a high-level objective that people won't embrace. In health care, making cost cutting or growth in market share the top priority is unlikely to resonate with caregivers whose passion is improving outcomes that matter to patients.

In our experience, every gritty health care organization has a primary goal of putting patients first. In fact, we believe a health care organization can't be gritty if it doesn't put that goal before everything else. Though it's challenging to suggest that other needs (such as those of doctors or researchers) come second or third, if patients' needs are not foremost, decisions tend to be based on politics rather than strategy as stakeholders jockey for resources. This doesn't mean an organization can't have other goals; Mayo, for instance, also values research, education, and public health. But those things are subordinate to patient care. (See figure 2.)

Of course, even when the high-level goal is clear and appropriate, rhetoric alone won't suffice to

FIGURE 2

Aligning organizational objectives

Gritty health care institutions have clear goal hierarchies, like the hypothetical schematic below. As with individual and team hierarchies, lower-level goals support those at the next tier, in service of a single, overarching top-level goal or mission.

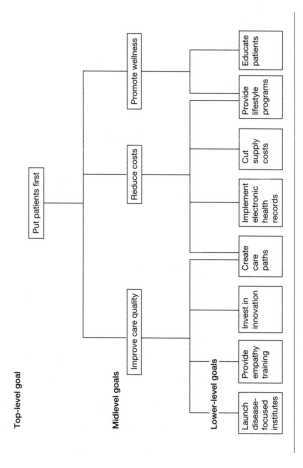

promote it—and can even backfire. If an organization's leaders don't use the goal to make decisions, it will undermine their credibility.

Consider how Cleveland Clinic responded when it learned that a delayed appointment had caused hours of suffering for a patient with difficulty urinating. The clinic began asking everyone requesting an appointment whether they wanted to be seen that day. Offering that option required complex and costly changes in how things were done, but it clearly put patients' needs first. As it happened, the change was rewarded with tremendous increases in market share, but this was a happy side effect, not the main intent of the change.

As this story shows, clarity around high-level goals can be a competitive differentiator in the market and have a valuable impact within the organization as well. Data from Press Ganey demonstrates that when clinicians and other employees embrace their organization's commitment to quality and safety, and when those goals reflect their own, it leads not only to better care but also to better business results.

But how can leaders help translate the top-level organizational goal into practical activities for teams and individuals? Seven years ago, Cleveland Clinic took an important step that helped define its culture and direction. Toby Cosgrove, the CEO at the time, had all employees engage in a half-day "appreciative inquiry" program, in which personnel in various roles sat at tables of about 10 and discussed cases in which the care a patient received had made them proud. The perspectives of physicians, nurses, janitors, and administrative staff were intertwined, and the focus was on positive real-life examples that captured Cleveland Clinic at its best.

The question posed was, "What made the care great in this instance, and how could Cleveland Clinic make that greatness happen every time?" The cost for taking its personnel offline for these exercises was estimated to be $11 million, but Cosgrove considers it one of the most powerful ways he helped the organization align around its mission.

Another tactic is to establish social norms that support the top-level goal. At Mayo Clinic, the social norm for clinicians is to respond to pages about patients immediately. They don't finish driving to their destination; they pull off the road and call in. They don't finish writing an email or conclude a conversation, even with a patient. They excuse themselves and answer the page.

"What happens if you don't answer your beeper right away?" we asked several people at Mayo. "You won't do well here," some told us. Another joked, "The earth will open up and swallow you." A third said, "The last thing you want is to have people say, 'He's the kind of guy who doesn't answer his page.'" It's part of a bigger picture. There is more to "the Mayo Way" than a dress code (and there is a dress code). It includes answering your beeper, working in teams, and putting patients' needs first.

Another fundamental characteristic of gritty organizations is restlessness with the status quo and an unrelenting drive to improve. Fostering that restlessness in a health care organization is a real test of leadership because health care is full of people who are well trained and work hard—but often are not receptive to hearing that change is needed. However, a goal of "preserving our greatness" is not a compelling argument for change or an attraction for gritty employees. The focus instead should be on health care's true customers—patients—not just on providing pleasant "service" but on the endless quest to meet their medical and emotional needs.

It also helps to promote inside the organization something Stanford psychologist Carol Dweck calls a *growth mindset*—a belief that abilities can be developed through hard work and feedback, and that major challenges and setbacks provide an opportunity to learn. That, of course, requires leadership to accept, and even publicly communicate, complications and errors—something that doesn't always come easily in health care. But leaders who are explicit about the need for calculated risk-taking, reducing mistakes, and continual learning tend to be the ones who actually inspire real growth in their organizations.

Crises offer special opportunities for growth—and in particular to strengthen culture. Organizations that have provided care after natural disasters or terrorist attacks have found that the experience leads to powerful bonding, a reinforced sense of purpose, the desire to excel, and a renewed commitment to organizational goals.

For example, when Hurricane Katrina hit New Orleans in 2005, a local hospital affiliated with Ochsner Health System faced a series of incredible challenges, including power outages, flooding, overcrowding, and inadequate food and supplies. But throughout, morale remained high because the employees all pulled together and performed duties outside their usual roles. Physicians served meals, for instance, and nurses cleaned units. "The team that was here throughout the storm has a relationship that can only be duplicated by soldiers in combat," the hospital's vice president of supply chain and support services told *Repertoire* magazine. "There's such respect and trust for one another."

Responding to self-generated crises can be a little trickier, however. But here, patient stories can be powerful drivers of improvement—especially if the stories are mortifying and involve "one of our own." At Henry Ford Health System, for example, every new employee watches a video depicting the experience of a physician in the system's intensive care unit, Rana Awdish, who nearly bled to death in the ICU in 2008 when a tumor in her liver suddenly ruptured. She was in severe shock and had a stroke; she was also seven months pregnant, and the baby did not survive.

As her conditioned worsened, Awdish heard her own colleagues say, "She's trying to die on us," and,

"She's circling the drain"—things that she herself had said when working in the same ICU. Hearing her describe her experience made her colleagues realize that her doctors were focused on the problem but not on her as a human being, and that this probably was happening a lot within Henry Ford. The crisis led leadership to commit to the goal of treating every patient with empathy all the time. Today every employee at Henry Ford has seen the video, and the goal of being reliably empathic is clearly understood. Sharing Awdish's story is just one of the interventions that has occurred at Henry Ford, and during the campaign that followed the organization saw most physician-related measures of patient experience improve by five to 10 percentage points.

The gritty leader

Ralph Waldo Emerson observed that organizations are the lengthened shadows of their leaders. To attract employees, build teams, and develop an organizational culture that all have grit, leaders should personify passion and perseverance—providing a visible, authoritative role model for every other person in the organization. And in their personal interactions, they too must be both demanding—keeping standards high—and supportive.

Consider Toby Cosgrove. He was a diligent student but, because he had dyslexia that was undiagnosed until his midthirties, his academic record was lackluster. Nevertheless, he set his sights on medical school, applying to 13. Just one, the University of Virginia, accepted him. In retrospect, "the dyslexia reinforced my determination and persistence," Cosgrove told us, "because I had to work more hours than anybody else to get the same result."

In 1968, Cosgrove's surgical residency was interrupted when he was drafted. He served a two-year tour as a U.S. Air Force surgeon in Vietnam. Upon his return home, he completed his residency and then joined Cleveland Clinic in 1975. "Everybody told me not to become a heart surgeon," he said. "I did it anyway." Indeed, Cosgrove performed more cardiac surgeries (about 22,000) than any of his contemporaries. He pioneered several technologies and innovations, including minimally invasive mitral valve surgery, earning more than 30 patents.

Cosgrove's development as a world-class surgeon is a case study in grit. "I was informed that I was the least talented individual in my residency. But failure is a great teacher. I worked and worked and worked at refining the craft," he told us. "I changed the way I did things over time. I used to take what I called 'innovation trips'—trips all over the world to watch other surgeons and their techniques. I'd pick things up from them and incorporate them in my practice. I was on a constant quest to find ways to do things better."

Cosgrove was named CEO of Cleveland Clinic in 2004. The passion and perseverance that made him great as a surgeon and as the head of a cardiac care team would soon be tested in his new role as leader of more than 43,000 employees. "I decided I had to become a student of leadership," Cosgrove recalls. "I had stacks of books on leadership, and every night when I came home, I would go up to my little office and read. And then I called up Harvard Business School professor Michael Porter." Porter, widely considered the father of the modern field of strategy, invited Cosgrove to visit. "He talked with me for two hours. After that, I got him to come to Cleveland. Since then, we've been sharing ideas," Cosgrove says. Porter helped him understand that as CEO he needed to be more than a renowned surgeon and an enthusiastic leader. He needed to evolve the organization's strategy, focusing on how to create value for patients and achieve competitive differentiation in the process.

Cosgrove scrutinized Cleveland Clinic's quality data; and while its mortality statistics were similar to those of other leading institutions, performance on other metrics—especially patient experience—left much to be desired. "People respected us," he says, "but they sure didn't like us." In 2009 he hired Jim Merlino, a young physician who had left the clinic unhappily after the death of his father there, and made him chief experience officer. Cosgrove asked Merlino to fix the things that had driven him away.

Cosgrove supported Merlino's many innovative ideas, including having all employees go through the appreciative inquiry exercise, and making an internal training film, an "empathy video" that is so powerful it has been watched by many outside the clinic, getting more than 4 million views on YouTube. As a result of these efforts and many others, Cleveland Clinic moved from the bottom quartile in patient experience to the top.

The institutional changes Cosgrove and his team have accomplished are too numerous to catalog, but here are a few: Swapping parking spaces so that patients, not doctors, are closest to the clinic's entrances. Moving medical records from hard copy to electronic storage. Developing standard care paths to ensure consistency and optimize the quality of care. Refusing to hire smokers and, recently, in response to the national opioid crisis, doing random drug testing of all Cleveland Clinic staff, including physicians and executives.

These changes weren't always popular when they were introduced. But when he knows he's right, Cosgrove stays the course. A placard he keeps on his desk reminds him "What can be conceived can be created."

It's hard to argue with the results achieved during his 13-year tenure as CEO. In addition to the improvements in patient experience, revenue grew from $3.7 billion in 2004 to $8.5 billion in 2016, and total annual visits increased from 2.8 million to 7.1 million. Quality on virtually every available metric has risen to the top tier of U.S. health care.

When Cosgrove gave his first big speech as CEO, he gave out 40,000 lapel buttons that said, "Patients First." We asked if some of his colleagues rolled their eyes. "Yes, a lot of them did," he said. "But I made the decision that I was going to pretend I didn't see them."

Cosgrove showed grit. And led an organization that has become his reflection.

THOMAS H. LEE is the chief medical officer of Press Ganey. He is also a professor of health policy and management at the Harvard T.H. Chan School of Public Health and a senior physician at Brigham and Women's Hospital. ANGELA DUCK-WORTH is the Rosa Lee and Egbert Chang Professor at the University of Pennsylvania and the Wharton School. She is also cofounder, chief scientist, and a board member of Character Lab, a nonprofit whose mission is to advance scientific insights that help children thrive.

Reprinted from *Harvard Business Review*,
September–October 2018 (product #R1805G).

Index

How to be human at work.

HBR's Emotional Intelligence Series features smart, essential reading on the human side of professional life from the pages of *Harvard Business Review*. Each book in the series offers uplifting stories, practical advice, and research from leading experts on how to tend to our emotional well-being at work.

Harvard Business Review Emotional Intelligence Series

Available in paperback or ebook format. The specially priced six-volume set includes:

- Mindfulness
- Resilience
- Influence and Persuasion
- Authentic Leadership
- Happiness
- Empathy